REV FR. DAVID LITTEL

Guardian Angel Novena

pocket Book

Contents

INTRODUCTION

The Role of Guardian Angels in Our Lives

Guardian Angels hold a significant and comforting role in the lives of believers. These celestial beings, assigned by God to each person, serve as protectors, guides, and messengers, reflecting God's care and love for humanity. Their presence is a testament to the divine concern for our spiritual and physical well-being, offering us constant companionship and assistance in our earthly journey.

1. Protectors

Guardian Angels are primarily known for their role in protecting us from physical and spiritual harm. They are vigilant in safeguarding us against dangers, whether they are immediate physical threats or more insidious spiritual attacks. This protective function is beautifully illustrated in Psalm 91:11-12: "For He will command His angels concerning you to guard you in all your ways; they will lift you up in their hands, so that you will not strike your foot against a stone."

2. Guides

In addition to protection, Guardian Angels offer guidance. They help direct our thoughts and actions towards God's will,

1

providing clarity in moments of confusion and strength in times of temptation. They assist us in discerning right from wrong and encourage us to choose paths that lead to spiritual growth and closer union with God. This guidance is akin to having a divine mentor who constantly steers us towards righteousness.

3. Messengers

Guardian Angels also act as messengers between God and humans. They deliver God's messages and bring our prayers and petitions to Him. This role is evident in the Annunciation, where the Angel Gabriel brings the message of Jesus' conception to Mary (Luke 1:26-38). Similarly, our Guardian Angels convey our needs and concerns to God, ensuring that our prayers are always heard.

4. Companions

Guardian Angels are our constant companions, never leaving our side from birth until death. Their unwavering presence reminds us that we are never alone, even in our darkest moments. This companionship offers immense comfort and encouragement, especially when we face challenges and feel isolated. Knowing that a divine friend is always with us can strengthen our faith and resolve.

5. Intercessors

Guardian Angels intercede on our behalf, praying for us and helping us in our spiritual battles. They are our advocates in the heavenly realm, always working for our good. This intercessory role is highlighted in the Book of Tobit, where the Archangel Raphael assists Tobit and his family (Tobit 12:12-15). Our Guardian Angels' prayers and support are invaluable in our journey toward salvation.

6. Witnesses of Our Lives

Guardian Angels witness every moment of our lives, sharing

in our joys and sorrows. They rejoice when we grow in virtue and grieve when we fall into sin. Their presence encourages us to live in a manner that honors God's love and grace, knowing that we are always observed and supported by these holy beings.

Conclusion

The role of Guardian Angels in our lives is multifaceted and deeply intertwined with our spiritual journey. They are protectors, guides, messengers, companions, intercessors, and witnesses, all dedicated to leading us closer to God. By recognizing and nurturing our relationship with our Guardian Angels, we can better appreciate the divine care that surrounds us and draw strength from their constant presence and support.

The Importance of a Novena

A novena, a nine-day period of prayer and devotion, holds a special place in the spiritual practices of many Christians. Rooted in the Latin word "novem," meaning "nine," a novena represents perseverance, faith, and the power of sustained prayer. It is a profound way to seek divine intervention, deepen one's faith, and foster a closer relationship with God and the saints.

1. Historical and Biblical Significance

The tradition of the novena has deep historical and biblical roots. One of the earliest examples is found in the Acts of the Apostles, where Mary and the apostles prayed together for nine days between Ascension and Pentecost, culminating in the descent of the Holy Spirit (Acts 1:12-14). This period of prayer highlights the importance of preparation and persistence in seeking God's will.

2. Spiritual Discipline and Commitment

Engaging in a novena requires discipline and commitment, reflecting a sincere desire to grow spiritually. The nine days of continuous prayer foster a habit of regular communication with God, strengthening one's faith and reliance on divine providence. This discipline helps believers to prioritize their spiritual life and maintain a steady focus on their relationship with God.

3. A Time for Reflection and Intention

Each day of a novena offers an opportunity for reflection and setting intentions. By focusing on a specific petition or theme, such as seeking guidance from a Guardian Angel, believers can delve deeper into their spiritual needs and aspirations. This intentional approach to prayer enhances the quality of one's spiritual life and encourages a deeper understanding of one's faith.

4. Community and Solidarity

Novenas are often prayed in community, bringing believers together in a shared spiritual journey. This communal aspect fosters a sense of solidarity and mutual support among participants, reinforcing the idea that we are all part of the Body of Christ. Praying together amplifies the power of the novena, as Jesus said, "For where two or three gather in my name, there am I with them" (Matthew 18:20).

5. Invoking the Intercession of Saints and Angels

A novena is a powerful way to invoke the intercession of saints and angels. By dedicating the prayer to a particular heavenly advocate, such as a Guardian Angel, believers can seek their guidance, protection, and assistance. This practice underscores the Catholic belief in the Communion of Saints and the supportive role that saints and angels play in our spiritual journey.

6. Building Faith and Hope

The structure of a novena, with its focused and repetitive nature, helps to build faith and hope in God's mercy and love. As believers commit to nine days of prayer, they cultivate a sense of trust in God's plan and a hopeful expectation of His intervention. This process can lead to profound spiritual experiences and answered prayers, reinforcing the efficacy of persistent prayer.

7. Healing and Transformation

Novenas can be a source of healing and transformation, providing comfort and strength in times of need. The act of consistently turning to God in prayer allows for personal growth, emotional healing, and spiritual renewal. By surrendering one's worries and desires to God over the course of nine days, believers can experience a deeper sense of peace and alignment with God's will.

Conclusion

The importance of a novena lies in its ability to deepen one's faith, foster spiritual discipline, and bring about personal and communal transformation. By committing to nine days of focused prayer, believers can draw closer to God, seek the intercession of saints and angels, and experience the power of sustained prayer. Whether prayed alone or in community, a novena is a profound spiritual practice that nurtures a deeper relationship with the divine.

How to Use This Book

Welcome to the Guardian Angel Novena. This book is designed to guide you through a nine-day journey of prayer, reflection, and spiritual growth. Whether you are new to the practice of novenas or have prayed many before, this guide aims to deepen your connection with your Guardian Angel and enrich your spiritual life.

S tructure of the Book
Each day of the novena is structured to provide a comprehensive and meaningful prayer experience. Here is how you can make the most of each section:

1. **Scripture Reading**

- Start each day with the provided scripture passage. Take a moment to read it slowly and attentively, allowing the words to resonate in your heart.
- Reflect on how the passage relates to the role and presence of your Guardian Angel.

1. **Meditation**

- After reading the scripture, move on to the meditation. This section offers insights and reflections on the day's theme.
- Spend a few minutes in silent contemplation, allowing the meditation to deepen your understanding and connection with your Guardian Angel.

1. **Prayer**

- The prayer for each day is a heartfelt plea for guidance,

protection, and intercession from your Guardian Angel.
· Pray earnestly, expressing your desires, concerns, and gratitude.

1. **Reflection**

· Each day ends with a reflection prompt. Use this space to journal your thoughts and feelings about the day's experience.
· Consider how the themes and insights of the day can be applied to your life.

Tips for a Fruitful Novena

1. **Set Aside Dedicated Time**

· Choose a specific time each day for your novena prayers. Consistency will help you build a habit and ensure that you complete the novena.

1. **Create a Sacred Space**

· Find a quiet, comfortable place where you can focus without distractions. Consider setting up a small altar with a candle, a Bible, and any religious images that inspire you.

1. **Be Open and Receptive**

· Approach each day with an open heart and mind. Be receptive to the messages and inspirations that come to you during your prayers and reflections.

1. **Stay Committed**

- If you miss a day, don't be discouraged. Simply continue where you left off, and try to maintain your commitment for the remainder of the novena.

1. **Share the Experience**

- If possible, share your novena journey with a friend or a prayer group. Discussing your insights and experiences can deepen your understanding and support your spiritual growth.

Additional Features

- **Conclusion**: At the end of the nine days, you will find a concluding section that provides guidance on continuing your relationship with your Guardian Angel.
- **Appendix**: The appendix includes additional prayers, the Litany of the Guardian Angels, and hymns that you can incorporate into your spiritual practice.

Getting Started

To begin your Guardian Angel Novena, simply turn to the first day's scripture reading. As you progress through the novena, allow yourself to be guided by the structure and prompts provided in this book. May this journey bring you closer to your Guardian Angel and enrich your spiritual life in profound ways.

Blessings on Your Journey

Remember, the purpose of this novena is to draw you closer to God through the intercession and companionship of your Guardian Angel. Embrace this time of prayer and reflection with faith and trust in God's loving presence in your life.

Day 1: The Presence of Guardian Angels

Scripture Reading: Psalm 91:11-12

F*or He will command His angels concerning you to guard you in all your ways; they will lift you up in their hands, so that you will not strike your foot against a stone.*

Meditation: The Ever-Present Help

As we embark on this novena, let us reflect on the comforting presence of our Guardian Angels. Psalm 91 assures us that God commands His angels to guard us in all our ways. This divine promise is a reminder that we are never alone. Our Guardian Angels are always with us, ready to protect and guide us through life's challenges.

Think about the times you felt an inexplicable sense of peace or narrowly avoided danger. These moments may have been the work of your Guardian Angel, quietly intervening on your behalf. Our angels are ever-present, lifting us up when we stumble and ensuring that we do not fall. They are God's gift to us, a manifestation of His unending love and care.

As we meditate on the presence of our Guardian Angels, let us open our hearts to recognize their influence in our lives. May this awareness bring us comfort and strengthen our faith in

God's providence.

Prayer

Heavenly Father, I thank You for the gift of my Guardian Angel. I am grateful for Your loving care and the protection You provide through Your angels. Today, I acknowledge the presence of my Guardian Angel in my life. I ask for the grace to be more aware of their guidance and protection.

Guardian Angel, my faithful companion, thank you for your constant watch over me. Help me to feel your presence and trust in your assistance. Guide my steps and keep me safe from harm. Lift me up when I am weary, and guard me in all my ways.

Lord, grant me the faith to trust in Your divine protection and the presence of my Guardian Angel. May this novena deepen my relationship with You and with the heavenly protector You have assigned to me. Amen.

Reflection

1. Reflect on a time when you felt protected or guided in an unexpected way. Could this have been the work of your Guardian Angel?
2. How can you become more aware of your Guardian Angel's presence in your daily life?
3. Take a moment to express gratitude for your Guardian Angel's constant vigilance and care.

Use this reflection time to journal your thoughts and feelings. Write down any insights or inspirations that come to you during your meditation and prayer. May this first day of the novena bring you closer to the divine presence that watches over you always.

Day 2: Trusting in Angelic Protection

Scripture Reading: Matthew 18:10

"*See that you do not despise one of these little ones. For I tell you that their angels in heaven always see the face of my Father in heaven.*"

Meditation: A Shield of Faith

Today, we focus on the trust we place in our Guardian Angels' protection. Jesus' words in Matthew 18:10 remind us of the special care and attention our angels have for us. They are always in the presence of God, interceding on our behalf and watching over us with divine vigilance.

Trust is a fundamental aspect of our faith. By trusting in the protection of our Guardian Angels, we affirm our belief in God's providence and His loving care. This trust allows us to face life's uncertainties with confidence, knowing that we are never alone and that we have powerful guardians by our side.

Consider the various ways in which you can strengthen your trust in your Guardian Angel. Reflect on past experiences where you felt their protection and guidance. Allow these memories to reinforce your faith and encourage you to rely more fully on their presence in your life.

Prayer

Heavenly Father, I come to You with a heart full of gratitude for the trust I can place in Your protection. Thank You for the gift of my Guardian Angel, who watches over me with unwavering care. Help me to grow in my trust and confidence in Your divine providence.

Guardian Angel, I entrust myself to your protection. Strengthen my faith and help me to remember that you are always with me, guiding and shielding me from harm. Give me the courage to face challenges with the assurance that you are by my side.

Lord, grant me the grace to trust in Your plan for my life. May this novena help me to deepen my faith and reliance on Your divine assistance. Amen.

Reflection

1. Reflect on the ways you have experienced your Guardian Angel's protection. How has this affected your trust in their presence?
2. In what areas of your life do you need to grow in trust and confidence in your Guardian Angel's protection?
3. Write down a prayer asking for increased trust and faith in your Guardian Angel's guidance and protection.

Use this reflection time to journal your thoughts and feelings. Write down any insights or inspirations that come to you during your meditation and prayer. May this second day of the novena strengthen your trust in the divine protection that surrounds you always.

Day 3: Guardian Angels as Messengers

Scripture Reading: Luke 1:26-38

I n the sixth month of Elizabeth's pregnancy, God sent the angel *Gabriel to Nazareth, a town in Galilee, to a virgin pledged to be married to a man named Joseph, a descendant of David. The virgin's name was Mary. The angel went to her and said, "Greetings, you who are highly favored! The Lord is with you."*

Meditation: Divine Communication

Today, we reflect on the role of Guardian Angels as messengers. The angel Gabriel's announcement to Mary is a profound example of how angels deliver divine messages. Just as Gabriel brought the message of Jesus' conception to Mary, our Guardian Angels communicate God's will and guidance to us.

Guardian Angels are entrusted with the task of delivering messages from God, providing us with direction and insight in our spiritual journey. They help us understand God's plan for our lives and offer us comfort and encouragement through their communications. By being attentive to their subtle guidance, we can align our actions with God's will.

Consider how you can become more attuned to the messages your Guardian Angel may be conveying. Reflect on moments of sudden clarity, unexpected wisdom, or inner peace. These may be instances of angelic communication meant to guide you on your path.

Prayer

Heavenly Father, I thank You for the gift of my Guardian Angel, who acts as Your messenger in my life. Help me to be attentive to the guidance and messages that my Guardian Angel brings. Open my heart and mind to discern Your will through their divine communication.

Guardian Angel, I am grateful for your constant watchfulness and the messages you bring from God. Help me to recognize and understand the guidance you offer. Give me the wisdom to follow the path that aligns with God's plan for me.

Lord, grant me the grace to be open and receptive to Your divine messages. May this novena help me to deepen my understanding and trust in Your communication through my Guardian Angel. Amen.

Reflection

1. Reflect on a time when you received unexpected guidance or insight. Could this have been a message from your Guardian Angel?
2. How can you become more attuned to the subtle messages your Guardian Angel may be conveying to you?
3. Write down a prayer asking for clarity and understanding in discerning the messages from your Guardian Angel.

Use this reflection time to journal your thoughts and feelings. Write down any insights or inspirations that come to you during your meditation and prayer. May this third day of the novena enhance your ability to recognize and respond to divine communication.

Day 4: Guardian Angels in Times of Trouble

Scripture Reading: Acts 12:5-11

So Peter was kept in prison, but the church was earnestly praying to God for him. The night before Herod was to bring him to trial, Peter was sleeping between two soldiers, bound with two chains, and sentries stood guard at the entrance. Suddenly an angel of the Lord appeared and a light shone in the cell. He struck Peter on the side and woke him up. "Quick, get up!" he said, and the chains fell off Peter's wrists. Then the angel said to him, "Put on your clothes and sandals." And Peter did so. "Wrap your cloak around you and follow me," the angel told him. Peter followed him out of the prison, but he had no idea that what the angel was doing was really happening; he thought he was seeing a vision. They passed the first and second guards and came to the iron gate leading to the city. It opened for them by itself, and they went through it. When they had walked the length of one street, suddenly the angel left him.

Meditation: Deliverance and Safety

Today, we focus on the role of Guardian Angels during times of trouble. The dramatic rescue of Peter by an angel is a powerful testament to the divine intervention that can occur in our darkest hours. Just as the angel freed Peter from prison, our Guardian Angels are present to help us through our own trials and tribulations.

In moments of fear, uncertainty, or danger, our Guardian Angels are there to offer support and protection. They can bring comfort and guidance, helping us to navigate through difficult situations. By placing our trust in their assistance, we can find strength and hope even in the most challenging times.

Reflect on your own experiences of trouble and how you may have felt a sense of divine help or comfort. Recognize the presence of your Guardian Angel during these times and invite their continued support and guidance.

Prayer

Heavenly Father, I thank You for the protection and deliverance provided by my Guardian Angel in times of trouble. I am grateful for Your constant care and the assurance that I am never alone, even in my darkest moments. Help me to trust in Your divine intervention and the presence of my Guardian Angel.

Guardian Angel, my protector and guide, I thank you for your steadfast presence during my times of trouble. Please continue to watch over me, offering support and guidance when I face challenges. Help me to feel your comforting presence and to trust in your ability to lead me to safety.

Lord, grant me the courage and faith to trust in Your divine help through my Guardian Angel. May this novena strengthen my reliance on Your protection and guidance in all circumstances. Amen.

Reflection

1. Reflect on a time when you faced significant trouble or

danger. How did you experience divine help or comfort during that time?

2. How can you cultivate a deeper trust in your Guardian Angel's protection during future challenges?

3. Write down a prayer asking for continued support and guidance from your Guardian Angel in times of trouble.

Use this reflection time to journal your thoughts and feelings. Write down any insights or inspirations that come to you during your meditation and prayer. May this fourth day of the novena reinforce your faith in the divine protection that is always available to you.

Day 5: Guidance from Guardian Angels

Scripture Reading: Exodus 23:20-22

"See, I am sending an angel ahead of you to guard you along the way and to bring you to the place I have prepared. Pay attention to him and listen to what he says. Do not rebel against him; he will not forgive your rebellion, since my Name is in him. If you listen carefully to what he says and do all that I say, I will be an enemy to your enemies and will oppose those who oppose you."*

Meditation: Walking the Right Path

Today, we reflect on the guidance our Guardian Angels provide. The passage from Exodus reminds us that God sends His angels to lead us along the path He has prepared for us. This divine guidance helps us navigate life's journey, making choices that align with God's will.

Guardian Angels serve as our heavenly guides, illuminating the way forward and helping us avoid spiritual pitfalls. By being attentive to their guidance, we can make decisions that honor God and lead us closer to Him. This requires a willingness to listen and a heart open to divine instruction.

Consider how you can be more receptive to the guidance of

your Guardian Angel. Reflect on moments when you felt a nudge or an inner conviction that directed you towards a better path. Acknowledge these instances as part of your angel's guidance and seek to be more attuned to their direction in the future.

Prayer

Heavenly Father, I thank You for the guidance You provide through my Guardian Angel. Help me to be attentive and obedient to the directions they give, so that I may walk the path You have prepared for me. Strengthen my faith and trust in Your divine plan.

Guardian Angel, my guide and protector, I am grateful for your constant watch over me. Help me to listen carefully to your guidance and to follow the path that leads to God. Give me the wisdom to discern your direction and the courage to act upon it.

Lord, grant me the grace to be receptive to Your guidance through my Guardian Angel. May this novena deepen my awareness of Your presence and lead me to a closer relationship with You. Amen.

Reflection

1. Reflect on a time when you felt guided in a particular direction. How did this experience impact your life and faith?
2. How can you become more attuned to the guidance of your Guardian Angel in your daily life?
3. Write down a prayer asking for clarity and discernment in following your Guardian Angel's guidance.

Use this reflection time to journal your thoughts and feelings. Write down any insights or inspirations that come to you during your meditation and prayer. May this fifth day of the novena enhance your ability to follow the divine guidance that leads you closer to God.

Day 6: Guardian Angels in Our Daily Lives

Scripture Reading: Hebrews 1:14

"*A*re not all angels ministering spirits sent to serve those who will inherit salvation?*"

Meditation: Constant Companionship

Today, we reflect on the presence of Guardian Angels in our daily lives. The scripture from Hebrews highlights the role of angels as ministering spirits sent by God to serve and assist us. Our Guardian Angels are always with us, offering constant companionship and support as we journey through life.

This ever-present companionship is a profound gift. It means that in every moment, whether mundane or significant, we are not alone. Our Guardian Angels are there to share in our joys, comfort us in our sorrows, and guide us in our decisions. Their presence is a testament to God's love and care, ensuring that we are always supported.

Consider the ways in which you can become more aware of your Guardian Angel's presence in your daily life. Reflect on the small, everyday moments where you might feel their influence and support. By acknowledging their constant companionship, you can foster a deeper sense of connection and gratitude.

Prayer

Heavenly Father, I thank You for the gift of my Guardian Angel, who is with me every moment of my life. Help me to become more aware of their presence and to appreciate the constant companionship they offer. May I always feel supported and loved by Your divine care.

Guardian Angel, my faithful companion, thank you for your unwavering presence in my life. Help me to recognize your support in my daily activities and to draw strength from knowing that you are always with me. Guide my steps and be my constant source of comfort and encouragement.

Lord, grant me the grace to live each day with the awareness of my Guardian Angel's presence. May this novena deepen my connection to You and to the heavenly companion You have assigned to me. Amen.

Reflection

1. Reflect on the everyday moments where you might feel your Guardian Angel's presence. How can this awareness impact your daily life and actions?
2. How can you cultivate a habit of acknowledging and appreciating your Guardian Angel's companionship throughout the day?
3. Write down a prayer expressing gratitude for your Guardian Angel's constant presence and asking for continued guidance and support.

Use this reflection time to journal your thoughts and feelings. Write down any insights or inspirations that come to you during your meditation and prayer. May this sixth day of the novena help you to fully embrace and appreciate the constant companionship of your Guardian Angel.

Day 7: Intercession of Guardian Angels

Scripture Reading: Tobit 12:12-15

"Wʜᴇɴ you and Sarah prayed, it was I who brought and read the record of your prayer before the glory of the Lord, and likewise whenever you would bury the dead. And that time when you did not hesitate to get up and leave your dinner to go and bury the dead, I was sent to test you. And at the same time God sent me to heal you and Sarah your daughter-in-law. I am Raphael, one of the seven angels who stand and serve before the glory of the Lord."

Meditation: Angels Carry Our Prayers

Today, we reflect on the intercessory role of Guardian Angels. The story of the Archangel Raphael in the Book of Tobit illustrates how angels not only protect and guide us but also carry our prayers to God. Our Guardian Angels are powerful intercessors, advocating for us and presenting our petitions before the throne of God.

Understanding this role can deepen our prayer life, knowing that our prayers are delivered by such faithful and powerful beings. Our Guardian Angels intercede for us, helping to bring our needs and desires before God in a way that aligns with His will. They understand our struggles and joys, and they fervently pray for our well-being and spiritual growth.

Reflect on the times you have sought divine help through prayer. Consider how your Guardian Angel has been involved in interceding on your behalf. Embrace this intercessory support and allow it to strengthen your trust in the power of prayer.

Prayer

Heavenly Father, I thank You for the intercession of my Guardian Angel, who carries my prayers to Your throne. I am grateful for their faithful service and the comfort of knowing that my petitions are heard and presented to You. Help me to trust in the power of their intercession.

Guardian Angel, my advocate and intercessor, thank you for your constant prayers on my behalf. Please continue to present my needs and desires to God, and intercede for me in all areas of my life. Help me to be patient and trust in God's perfect timing and will.

Lord, grant me the grace to be persistent in prayer and to rely on the intercession of my Guardian Angel. May this novena deepen my faith and trust in Your divine providence. Amen.

Reflection

1. Reflect on a time when you felt your prayers were answered in a significant way. How does this reinforce your faith in the intercession of your Guardian Angel?
2. How can you incorporate the awareness of your Guardian Angel's intercession into your daily prayer routine?
3. Write down a prayer asking for continued intercession from your Guardian Angel and expressing trust in their advocacy before God.

Use this reflection time to journal your thoughts and feelings. Write down any insights or inspirations that come to you during your meditation and prayer. May this seventh day of the novena deepen your trust in the powerful intercession of your Guardian Angel.

Day 8: Gratitude for Guardian Angels

Scripture Reading: Psalm 34:7

"T he angel of the Lord encamps around those who fear him, and he delivers them."

Meditation: Thankfulness and Praise

Today, we focus on expressing gratitude for the presence and assistance of our Guardian Angels. The verse from Psalm 34 reminds us of the protective and delivering role that angels play in our lives. Recognizing their constant care and guidance invites us to cultivate a heart full of thankfulness and praise.

Gratitude is a powerful spiritual practice. By acknowledging the ways in which our Guardian Angels support and protect us, we can deepen our appreciation for God's provision and care. This gratitude not only honors our angels but also enhances our overall spiritual well-being, fostering a closer relationship with God.

Reflect on the many blessings and protections you have received through the intervention of your Guardian Angel. Take time to offer sincere thanks for their unwavering presence and the numerous ways they have assisted you throughout your life.

Prayer

Heavenly Father, I thank You for the gift of my Guardian Angel and for the countless ways they have protected and guided me. I am grateful for Your provision and care, manifested through the constant presence of my Guardian Angel. Help me to cultivate a heart full of gratitude and praise.

Guardian Angel, I thank you for your unwavering vigilance and assistance. Thank you for guarding me, guiding me, and interceding on my behalf. Help me to always recognize and appreciate your presence in my life.

Lord, grant me the grace to live each day with a spirit of thankfulness. May this novena deepen my gratitude for the divine care I receive through my Guardian Angel. Amen.

Reflection

1. Reflect on specific instances where you have felt the protection and guidance of your Guardian Angel. How have these experiences impacted your faith and gratitude?
2. How can you regularly incorporate expressions of gratitude for your Guardian Angel into your prayer life?
3. Write down a prayer of thanksgiving for the presence and assistance of your Guardian Angel, expressing specific reasons for your gratitude.

Use this reflection time to journal your thoughts and feelings. Write down any insights or inspirations that come to you during your meditation and prayer. May this eighth day of the novena fill your heart with gratitude and praise for the constant care of your Guardian Angel.

Day 9: Renewing Our Commitment to God

Scripture Reading: Revelation 5:11-12

"Then I looked and heard the voice of many angels, numbering thousands upon thousands, and ten thousand times ten thousand. They encircled the throne and the living creatures and the elders. In a loud voice they were saying: 'Worthy is the Lamb, who was slain, to receive power and wealth and wisdom and strength and honor and glory and praise!'"

Meditation: Worship with the Angels

As we conclude this novena, let us reflect on our commitment to God and the example of the angels who worship Him unceasingly. The vision in Revelation gives us a glimpse of the heavenly worship where countless angels praise God. This celestial worship reminds us of our ultimate purpose: to glorify God with our lives.

Our Guardian Angels continually worship and adore God, and they encourage us to do the same. By renewing our commitment to God, we align ourselves with the divine purpose and join the angels in their eternal praise. This renewal involves deepening our faith, increasing our trust in God's plan, and living a life that reflects His love and grace.

Consider how you can renew your commitment to God today. Reflect on the insights and spiritual growth you have experienced during this novena. Let this be a moment to rededicate yourself to God's service and to live in a way that honors Him and follows His guidance.

Prayer

Heavenly Father, I thank You for the journey of this novena and for the presence of my Guardian Angel. I am grateful for the protection, guidance, and intercession I have received. Today, I renew my commitment to You, inspired by the example of the angels who worship You continually.

Guardian Angel, thank you for leading me closer to God and for your constant care. Help me to live a life that reflects God's love and glory. Guide my actions and decisions so that they honor God and align with His will.

Lord, grant me the grace to renew my commitment to You each day. May my life be a testament to Your love and a reflection of the worship offered by the angels. Strengthen my faith and help me to trust in Your divine plan. Amen.

Reflection

1. Reflect on the spiritual insights and growth you have experienced during this novena. How have these moments brought you closer to God and your Guardian Angel?

2. How can you renew your commitment to God in your daily life? What specific actions can you take to live more faithfully?

3. Write down a prayer of rededication, expressing your renewed commitment to God and your desire to live in a way that honors Him.

Use this reflection time to journal your thoughts and feelings. Write down any insights or inspirations that come to you during your meditation and prayer. May this final day of the novena strengthen your commitment to God and deepen your relationship with your Guardian Angel.

Prayers to Guardian Angels

Daily Prayer to Your Guardian Angel

Angel of God, my guardian dear, To whom God's love commits me here, Ever this day, be at my side, To light and guard, to rule and guide. Amen.

Prayer for Guidance

O Holy Guardian Angel, Take care of my soul and body. Enlighten my mind so that I may know the Lord better And love Him with all my heart. Help me in my prayers so that I may not give in to distractions. Assist me with your advice, So that I may see the good and carry it out with generosity. Defend me from the insidious snares of the enemy, And sustain me in temptations that I may always be strong in faith. Intercede for me with the Lord. Teach me to be docile to the inspirations of the Holy Spirit. Cover me with your protecting wings, And let me become a docile instrument in God's hands. I ask all this through Christ, our Lord. Amen.

Prayer for Protection

O Angel of God, appointed by His divine mercy to be my guardian, Enlighten and protect me, direct and govern me this day. Amen.

Litany of the Guardian Angels

Lord, have mercy on us. Christ, have mercy on us. Lord, have mercy on us. Christ, hear us. Christ, graciously hear us.

God the Father of Heaven, Have mercy on us. **God the Son, Redeemer of the world,** Have mercy on us. **God the Holy Spirit,** Have mercy on us. **Holy Trinity, One God,** Have mercy on us.

Holy Mary, Queen of Angels, Pray for us. **Holy Guardian Angels,** Pray for us.

Holy Guardian Angels, who never leave our side, Pray for us. **Holy Guardian Angels, who are devoted to us in Heavenly friendship,** Pray for us. **Holy Guardian Angels, our faithful admonishers,** Pray for us. **Holy Guardian Angels, our wise counselors,** Pray for us. **Holy Guardian Angels, who preserve us from many evils of body and soul,** Pray for us. **Holy Guardian Angels, our mighty defenders against the attacks of the evil one,** Pray for us. **Holy Guardian Angels, our support in times of temptation,** Pray for us. **Holy Guardian Angels, who help us when we stumble and fall,** Pray for us. **Holy Guardian Angels, who comfort us in troubles and sufferings,** Pray for us. **Holy Guardian Angels, who carry our prayers to the throne of God,** Pray for us. **Holy Guardian Angels, who bring us the assistance of Heaven,** Pray for us. **Holy Guardian Angels, who exhort us to faith, hope, and charity,** Pray for us. **Holy Guardian Angels, our wise and faithful guides,** Pray for us. **Holy Guardian Angels, who help us to persevere in holiness,** Pray for us. **Holy Guardian Angels, who lead us safely to the gates of Heaven,** Pray for us. **Holy Guardian Angels, who we shall one day behold face to face,** Pray for us. **Holy Guardian Angels, whom we venerate and love now as our protectors,** Pray for us.

Lamb of God, who takes away the sins of the world, Spare us, O Lord. **Lamb of God, who takes away the sins of the world,** Graciously hear us, O Lord. **Lamb of God, who takes away the sins of the world,** Have mercy on us.

Lord, have mercy on us. Christ, have mercy on us. Lord, have mercy on us.

Pray for us, O Holy Guardian Angels, That we may be made worthy of the promises of Christ.

Let Us Pray:

Almighty and eternal God, who in Your immense goodness has given us the holy angels to guard us, grant that we, Your supplicants, may be always defended by their protection and may rejoice eternally in their company. Through Christ our Lord. Amen.

Hymns and Songs

Hymn: "Angel of God"

1. Angel of God, my guardian dear, To whom God's love commits me here, Ever this day, be at my side, To light and guard, to rule and guide.

Refrain: Angel of God, be my light, Guide and protect me day and night.

1. In times of trouble, be my aid, Your gentle wings will be my shade. When danger comes, I shall not fear, For you, my angel, will be near.

Refrain: Angel of God, be my light, Guide and protect me day and night.

1. In daily life, as I proceed, Your guidance, Lord, is all I need. My guardian angel, friend and guide, In God's love, we'll abide.

Refrain: Angel of God, be my light, Guide and protect me day and night.

Hymn: "Holy Angels Bright"

1. Holy angels bright, Who wait at God's right hand, Or through the realms of light Fly at your Lord's command, Assist our song, For else the theme Too high doth seem For mortal tongue.
2. You blessed souls at rest, Who ran this earthly race And now, from sin released, Behold the Savior's face, God's praises sound, As in His sight With sweet delight You do abound.
3. Let us who toil below Adore our heavenly King, And onward as we go Our joyful anthems sing; With one accord, Through good or ill, We'll praise Him still, Eternal Lord.
4. My soul, bear thou thy part, Triumph in God above, And with a well-tuned heart Sing thou the songs of love! Let all thy days Till life shall end, Whate'er He send, Be filled with praise.

These prayers, litanies, and hymns are meant to enrich your devotional practices and deepen your connection with your Guardian Angel. May they bring you closer to the divine presence and protection that surrounds you always.

9-Day Devotional to Your Guardian Angel

I ntroduction
   Welcome to the 9-Day Devotional to Your Guardian Angel, a spiritual journey designed to deepen your relationship with the angelic protector God has assigned to you. Through daily prayers, scripture readings, and reflections, you will explore the vital role of your Guardian Angel and learn to trust in their guidance, protection, and companionship.

Day 1: Trusting in Your Guardian Angel

Opening Prayer

In the name of the Father, and of the Son, and of the Holy Spirit. Amen.

Heavenly Father, as we begin this devotional, we ask for Your grace and guidance. Help us to trust in the presence and protection of our Guardian Angels. Amen.

Scripture Reading: Psalm 91:11-12

"For he will command his angels concerning you to guard you in all your ways; they will lift you up in their hands, so that you will not strike your foot against a stone."

Reflection

Your Guardian Angel is always with you, watching over you and protecting you from harm. Trusting in their presence can bring great comfort and reassurance. Take time today to acknowledge your Guardian Angel and thank them for their constant care.

Devotional Prayer

Dear Guardian Angel, I trust in your presence and protection. Help me to feel your guidance and support in my daily life. Thank you for watching over me and keeping me safe. Amen.

Personal Intentions

(Here, you can silently mention your specific prayers and intentions.)

Closing Prayer

Heavenly Father, we thank You for the gift of Guardian Angels. Help us to trust in their presence and protection. We ask this through Christ our Lord. Amen.

In the name of the Father, and of the Son, and of the Holy Spirit. Amen.

Day 2: Seeking Guidance and Protection

Opening Prayer

In the name of the Father, and of the Son, and of the Holy Spirit. Amen.

Heavenly Father, as we continue this devotional, we ask for Your guidance and protection through our Guardian Angels. Amen.

Scripture Reading: Exodus 23:20

"See, I am sending an angel ahead of you to guard you along the way and to bring you to the place I have prepared."

Reflection

Your Guardian Angel is sent by God to guide and protect you on your journey. Trust in their guidance and seek their protection in all that you do. Know that they are with you, helping you to reach the place God has prepared for you.

Devotional Prayer

Dear Guardian Angel, guide me and protect me on my journey. Help me to follow God's path and to reach the place He has prepared for me. Thank you for your constant presence and care. Amen.

Personal Intentions

(Here, you can silently mention your specific prayers and intentions.)

Closing Prayer

Heavenly Father, we thank You for the guidance and protection of our Guardian Angels. Help us to trust in their presence and to follow their guidance. We ask this through Christ our Lord. Amen.

In the name of the Father, and of the Son, and of the Holy Spirit. Amen.

Day 3: Strengthening Faith and Courage

Opening Prayer

In the name of the Father, and of the Son, and of the Holy Spirit. Amen.

Heavenly Father, as we continue this devotional, we ask for the strength and courage to face our challenges with the help of our Guardian Angels. Amen.

Scripture Reading: Daniel 6:22

"My God sent his angel, and he shut the mouths of the lions.

They have not hurt me, because I was found innocent in his sight."

Reflection

God sends His angels to give us strength and courage in times of trial. Just as Daniel was protected in the lion's den, we can trust that our Guardian Angels will help us face our challenges with faith and bravery.

Devotional Prayer

Dear Guardian Angel, give me the strength and courage to face my challenges. Help me to trust in God's protection and to stand firm in my faith. Thank you for being by my side. Amen.

Personal Intentions

(Here, you can silently mention your specific prayers and intentions.)

Closing Prayer

Heavenly Father, we thank You for the strength and courage our Guardian Angels provide. Help us to trust in their protection and to stand firm in our faith. We ask this through Christ our Lord. Amen.

In the name of the Father, and of the Son, and of the Holy Spirit. Amen.

Day 4: Embracing God's Will

Opening Prayer

In the name of the Father, and of the Son, and of the Holy Spirit. Amen.

Heavenly Father, as we continue this devotional, we ask for the grace to embrace Your will, guided by our Guardian Angels. Amen.

Scripture Reading: Matthew 26:53

"Do you think I cannot call on my Father, and he will at once put at my disposal more than twelve legions of angels?"

Reflection

Jesus trusted in God's will, knowing that angels were ready to assist Him. We too can trust in God's plan for our lives, knowing that our Guardian Angels are with us to guide and support us in following His will.

Devotional Prayer

Dear Guardian Angel, help me to embrace God's will for my life. Guide me in following His plan and trusting in His wisdom. Thank you for your constant presence and support. Amen.

Personal Intentions

(Here, you can silently mention your specific prayers and intentions.)

Closing Prayer

Heavenly Father, we thank You for the guidance of our Guardian Angels in embracing Your will. Help us to trust in Your plan and to follow it faithfully. We ask this through Christ our Lord. Amen.

In the name of the Father, and of the Son, and of the Holy Spirit. Amen.

Day 5: Overcoming Temptations

Opening Prayer

In the name of the Father, and of the Son, and of the Holy Spirit. Amen.

Heavenly Father, as we continue this devotional, we ask for the strength to overcome temptations with the help of our Guardian Angels. Amen.

Scripture Reading: 1 Corinthians 10:13

"No temptation has overtaken you except what is common to mankind. And God is faithful; he will not let you be tempted beyond what you can bear. But when you are tempted, he will also provide a way out so that you can endure it."

Reflection

God provides us with the strength to overcome temptations, often through the guidance and protection of our Guardian Angels. Trust in their help to resist temptation and to follow the path of righteousness.

Devotional Prayer

Dear Guardian Angel, help me to overcome temptations and to stay on the path of righteousness. Give me the strength to resist and to follow God's will. Thank you for your guidance and protection. Amen.

Personal Intentions

(Here, you can silently mention your specific prayers and intentions.)

Closing Prayer

Heavenly Father, we thank You for the strength to overcome temptations, provided through our Guardian Angels. Help us to trust in their guidance and to remain faithful to You. We ask this through Christ our Lord. Amen.

In the name of the Father, and of the Son, and of the Holy Spirit. Amen.

Day 6: Finding Peace and Comfort

Opening Prayer

In the name of the Father, and of the Son, and of the Holy Spirit. Amen.

Heavenly Father, as we continue this devotional, we ask for

peace and comfort through the presence of our Guardian Angels. Amen.

Scripture Reading: Psalm 34:7

"The angel of the Lord encamps around those who fear him, and he delivers them."

Reflection

Your Guardian Angel is always near, offering peace and comfort in times of trouble. Trust in their presence and allow them to bring you God's peace and reassurance.

Devotional Prayer

Dear Guardian Angel, bring me peace and comfort in times of trouble. Help me to trust in your presence and to feel God's peace in my heart. Thank you for your constant care. Amen.

Personal Intentions

(Here, you can silently mention your specific prayers and intentions.)

Closing Prayer

Heavenly Father, we thank You for the peace and comfort our Guardian Angels provide. Help us to trust in their presence and to feel Your peace in our hearts. We ask this through Christ our Lord. Amen.

In the name of the Father, and of the Son, and of the Holy Spirit. Amen.

Day 7: Developing a Deeper Prayer Life

Opening Prayer

In the name of the Father, and of the Son, and of the Holy Spirit. Amen.

Heavenly Father, as we continue this devotional, we ask for the grace to develop a deeper prayer life with the guidance of our Guardian Angels. Amen.

Scripture Reading: Acts 12:7-10

"Suddenly an angel of the Lord appeared and a light shone in the cell. He struck Peter on the side and woke him up. 'Quick, get up!' he said, and the chains fell off Peter's wrists. Then the angel said to him, 'Put on your clothes and sandals.' And Peter did so. 'Wrap your cloak around you and follow me,' the angel told him. Peter followed him out of the prison."

Reflection

Your Guardian Angel can help you develop a deeper prayer life, guiding you in your communication with God. Trust in their guidance and seek their help in deepening your relationship with the Lord through prayer.

Devotional Prayer

Dear Guardian Angel, guide me in developing a deeper prayer life. Help me to communicate with God more intimately and to grow closer to Him. Thank you for your guidance and support. Amen.

Personal Intentions

(Here, you can silently mention your specific prayers and intentions.)

Closing Prayer

Heavenly Father, we thank You for the guidance of our Guardian Angels in developing a deeper prayer life. Help us to grow closer to You through prayer. We ask this through Christ our Lord. Amen.

In the name of the Father, and of the Son, and of the Holy Spirit. Amen.

Day 8: Trusting in Divine Providence

Opening Prayer

In the name of the Father, and of the Son, and of the Holy Spirit. Amen.

Heavenly Father, as we continue this devotional, we ask for the grace to trust in Your divine providence with the help of our Guardian Angels. Amen.

Scripture Reading: Matthew 18:10

"See that you do not despise one of these little ones. For I tell you that their angels in heaven always see the face of my Father in heaven."

Reflection

Trusting in God's divine providence means believing that He is always watching over you and guiding you through His angels. Your Guardian Angel is a sign of God's care and a reminder that you are never alone.

Devotional Prayer

Dear Guardian Angel, help me to trust in God's divine providence. Remind me that God is always watching over me and guiding me through you. Thank you for your constant presence and care. Amen.

Personal Intentions

(Here, you can silently mention your specific prayers and intentions.)

Closing Prayer

Heavenly Father, we thank You for the assurance of Your divine providence through our Guardian Angels. Help us to trust in Your care and guidance. We ask this through Christ our Lord. Amen.

In the name of the Father, and of the Son, and of the Holy

Spirit. Amen.

Day 9: Gratitude for Your Guardian Angel

Opening Prayer

In the name of the Father, and of the Son, and of the Holy Spirit. Amen.

Heavenly Father, as we conclude this devotional, we thank You for the gift of our Guardian Angels. Help us to live in gratitude for their constant presence and protection. Amen.

Scripture Reading: Hebrews 1:14

"Are not all angels ministering spirits sent to serve those who will inherit salvation?"

Reflection

Your Guardian Angel is a gift from God, sent to guide, protect, and support you throughout your life. Take time today to express your gratitude for their constant presence and care.

Devotional Prayer

Dear Guardian Angel, I thank you for your constant presence and protection. Help me to live in gratitude for your guidance and care. May I always appreciate the gift that you are in my life. Amen.

Personal Intentions

(Here, you can silently mention your specific prayers and intentions.)

Closing Prayer

Heavenly Father, we thank You for the gift of our Guardian Angels. Help us to live in gratitude for their constant presence and protection. We ask this through Christ our Lord. Amen.

In the name of the Father, and of the Son, and of the Holy Spirit. Amen.

Conclusion

Reflecting on the presence and guidance of your Guardian Angel through this 9-day devotional can bring comfort, strength, and a deeper connection to God. May you continue to feel the support and protection of your Guardian Angel in all aspects of your life.

Conclusion

As you conclude this novena, take a moment to reflect on the spiritual journey you have undertaken. Over the past nine days, you have deepened your connection with your Guardian Angel, explored their roles and presence in your life, and experienced the power of sustained prayer and reflection. This is not the end, but rather the beginning of an ongoing relationship with your Guardian Angel and a continued commitment to your spiritual growth.

Continuing Your Relationship with Your Guardian Angel

Maintaining a close relationship with your Guardian Angel involves integrating the lessons and practices from this novena into your daily life. Here are some ways to continue nurturing this divine connection:

1. Daily Prayer

Make it a habit to include a prayer to your Guardian Angel in your daily routine. This can be as simple as the traditional "Angel of God" prayer or a personal invocation for guidance and protection.

2. Attentiveness to Guidance

Stay attentive to the subtle signs and promptings from your Guardian Angel. This may come through inner convictions, dreams, or unexpected insights. Trust in their guidance and be open to their influence.

3. Gratitude and Acknowledgment

Regularly express your gratitude for your Guardian Angel's presence and assistance. Acknowledge their role in your life, especially during times of protection, guidance, and intercession.

4. Devotional Practices

Incorporate devotions to your Guardian Angel into your spiritual practices. This could include specific prayers, litanies, or hymns dedicated to your Guardian Angel.

Additional Prayers and Devotions

Prayer of Thanksgiving

Heavenly Father, I thank You for the gift of my Guardian Angel. I am grateful for their constant presence, guidance, and protection. Help me to remain aware of their influence in my life and to respond with trust and obedience. Guardian Angel, I thank you for your faithful service and devotion. Continue to guide and protect me as I seek to follow God's will. Amen.

Night Prayer to Your Guardian Angel

Angel of God, my guardian dear, To whom God's love commits me here, Ever this night, be at my side, To light and guard, to rule and guide. Amen.

Prayer for Discernment

O Holy Guardian Angel, Illuminate my mind with the light of God, Guide my heart to seek His will, And strengthen my spirit to follow His path. Help me to discern the choices that lead to holiness And grant me the wisdom to avoid the pitfalls of sin. In all things, may I trust in your guidance And remain faithful to God's divine plan. Amen.

Resources for Further Reading

To continue your spiritual journey and deepen your understanding of Guardian Angels and their role in your life, consider exploring the following resources:

Books

- **"Angels and Saints: A Biblical Guide to Friendship with God's Holy Ones"** by Scott Hahn
- **"The Angels: In Catholic Teaching and Tradition"** by Fr. Pascale Parente
- **"All About the Angels"** by Fr. Paul O'Sullivan

Online Resources

- **EWTN's Angelology Section:** EWTN Angels
- **Catholic Answers on Angels:** Catholic Answers Angels
- **Vatican's Teachings on Angels:** Vatican Angels

Prayer Apps

- **Laudate:** An all-in-one Catholic app with prayers, daily readings, and more.
- **Hallow:** A Catholic prayer and meditation app that includes angelic prayers and devotions.

By continuing to nurture your relationship with your Guardian Angel, you can experience ongoing spiritual growth and a deeper connection with God's divine presence in your life. May your Guardian Angel always guide, protect, and inspire you as you journey in faith.

Made in the USA
Middletown, DE
04 September 2024